If There Were Dreams to Sell

Compiled by Barbara Lalicki

Illustrated by Margot Tomes

LOTHROP, LEE & SHEPARD BOOKS   NEW YORK

A B C D E

Z

Y

X

Library of Congress Cataloging in Publication Data
Lalicki, Barbara.
    If there were dreams to sell.
    Summary: Each letter of the alphabet is accompanied
by an illustration and appropriate poem or a phrase from a poem.
    1. English language—Alphabet—Juvenile literature.
2. Children's poetry. [1. Alphabet.   2. Poetry—
Collections]   I. Tomes, Margot, ill.   II. Title.
PE1155.L3   1984   821'.008'09282   [E]   84-907
ISBN 0-688-03821-2
ISBN 0-688-03822-0 (lib. bdg.)

Design and calligraphy by Julie Y. Quan

W V U T S

F G H I J

K

L

M

For my parents, James and Mary Stupple
~ BSL

For Betty Main
~ MT

R Q P O N

Apple

Hail to thee, old apple tree!

From every bough

Give us apples enow;

Hatsful, capsful,

Bushel, bushel, sacksful

And our arms full, too.

a

Bee

Oh, for a bee's experience
Of clovers and of noon!

b

Cow

High diddle, diddle,

The Cat and the Fiddle,

    The Cow jumped over the Moon;

The little Dog laughed

To see such Sport,

    And the Dish ran away with the Spoon.

C

DREAMS

If there were dreams to sell,
What would you buy?

E LVES

I count eleven

Airy elves by moonlight shadow seen.

e

F ROST

The Frost performs its secret ministry
Unhelped by any wind.

f

GHOSTS

GOBLINS

GREMLINS

g

HALLOWEEN

Hark, hark, the dogs do bark,
The beggars are coming to town;
Some in jags, and some in rags,
And some in velvet gowns.

Some gave them white bread
And some gave them brown,
And some gave them a good horse-whip,
And sent them out of town.

h

I

I had a little pony,

His name was Dapple Gray;

I lent him to a lady

To ride a mile away.

She whipped him, she lashed him,

She rode him through the mire;

I would not lend my pony now,
For all the lady's hire.

i

JOURNEY

One of the pleasantest things in the world is going on a journey; but I like to go by myself.

j

K ITE

k

LEAF

The one red leaf, the last of its clan,

That dances as often as dance it can,

Hanging so light, and hanging so high,

On the topmost twig that looks up at the sky.

1

Moon

The man in the moon
Came tumbling down,
And ask'd his way to Norwich,
He went by the south,
And burnt his mouth,
With supping hot pease porridge.

m

N IGHT

n

O WL

In an oak there liv'd an owl,
Frisky, whisky, wheedle!
She thought herself a clever fowl,
Fiddle, faddle, feedle!

O

P USSYCAT

Pussycat, wussycat, with a white foot,

When is your wedding, and I'll come to it.

The beer's to brew, the bread's to bake,

Pussycat, pussycat, don't be late!

p

Q

QUEEN

1. The Queen of Hearts
   She made some tarts,
   All on a summer's day;

3. The King of Hearts
   Called for the tarts,
   And beat the Knave full sore;

q

R ASPBERRY TARTS

2. The knave of Hearts

He stole the tarts,

And took them clean away.

4. The Knave of Hearts

Brought back the tarts,

And vow'd he'd steal no more.

Recipe
(makes 12 cookies)

Heat oven to 325 degrees.

1¼ C. unsalted butter, softened
⅔ C. sugar
2 C. sifted flour
1¾ C. finely-ground almonds
(about 5 oz. of slivered nuts)
⅛ tsp. cinnamon
5 Tbsp. raspberry jam

Cream the butter and sugar until light and fluffy. Then beat in the flour, ½ C. at a time, and the almonds and cinnamon. Shape the slightly stiff dough into a ball, wrap in plastic wrap, and refrigerate 1 hour. Then roll dough into a sheet ⅛ inch thick. Cut as many hearts as you can with a 2½-inch heart-shaped cutter. Knead, roll, and cut again. When you have 12 hearts, place them on an ungreased cookie sheet. Repeat the rolling and cutting, this time cutting out the center with a ½-inch round cutter. Bake for 15 to 20 minutes or until light brown. Remove cookies from sheets. Cool 20 minutes. Spread top of solid hearts with raspberry jam; press a heart with a cutout on top of each. Spoon a dab of jam into each hole, and enjoy!

r

Song

...just hear the little birdie's song!

A sound like honey

streaming through the woods.

S

T ROLL

The Troll went on to the market-place
    and peeped above the stalls;
the sheep went wild when they saw his face
    and the geese flew over the walls.

t

U NDER

Under the spreading chestnut-tree
  The village smithy stands;
The smith, a mighty man is he,
  With large and sinewy hands
. . . .
Week in, week out, from morn till night,
  You can hear his bellows blow;
You can hear him swing his heavy sledge,
  With measured beat and slow,
Like a sexton ringing the village bell,
  When the evening sun is low.

u

K Once a common bird in England, the kite has long wings and a forked tail. The toy's flight reminded people of the bird's flight, and so was called a kite, too.

L Samuel Taylor Coleridge. There really was a red leaf, as we can tell by Dorothy Wordsworth's journal entry for March 1, 1798: "William and I drank tea at Coleridge's. A cloudy sky. Observed nothing particularly interesting—the distant prospect obscured. One only leaf upon the top of a tree—the sole remaining leaf—danced round and round like a rag blown by the wind." It is fascinating to see how Coleridge used this vision in "Christabel."

M-Q The selections are from Mother Goose. Read "M" so that *Nor'ich* rhymes with *por'ich*. The pussycat shown for "P" is the artist's own Frith.

R Claire Counihan's raspberry tarts are delicious. She suggests using a spatula to slide the cookie dough onto the baking sheets, and recommends cookie cutters with scalloped edges. She often adds more ground nuts to bring out the almond flavor, and urges readers to use a fine jam made solely of raspberries and sugar, with no pectin to mask the raspberry taste.

S Aristophanes. From William Arrowsmith's translation of *The Birds*.

T J. R. R. Tolkien. From *Adventures of Tom Bombadil*, "Perry the Winkle," by J. R. R. Tolkien, published by George Allen & Unwin Ltd., England.

U & V Henry Wadsworth Longfellow. The poet, who had six children of his own, included these lines in "The Village Blacksmith": "And children coming home from school/Look in at the open door,/They love to see the flaming forge,/And hear the bellows roar,/And catch the burning sparks that fly/Like chaff from a threshing-floor."

W Alfred, Lord Tennyson. From "In Memoriam." The whole stanza reads: "Ring out, wild bells, to the wild sky,/The flying cloud, the frosty light:/The year is dying in the night/Ring out, wild bells, and let him die."

X American newspapers. It seems that this phrase should predate the alphabet, but it originated in American newspaper photo captions and caught on with the public. It was widely used in speech by the late 1920s, according to Eric Partridge, author of *A Dictionary of Catch Phrases*, A Scarborough Book, published by Stein & Day.

Y John Donne. From "Song." This pretty word is now archaic, but perhaps you will find a time to use it. Samuel Johnson defines *yesternight* as "on the night of yesterday, last night."

Z John Keats. From the sonnet "Oh! How I love!" "The frolic wind that breathes the Spring," wrote John Milton in "L'Allegro." Zephyrus is the god of the west wind.

ABOUT THE SELECTIONS

A Anonymous. To celebrate Twelfth Night, on January 5, people gathered around the oldest or most fruitful tree in the orchard. With a fruit drink called wassail (wäs-əl) in hand, they'd dance around the tree and sing this song. Readers will easily guess that *enow* means "enough." To the medieval wassailers, it also meant "by and by," and this may have been a part of the song's meaning.

"The purpose of this amusing, noisy ritual is to ensure plenty of good cider to fill the cups next year. Wassailing fruit trees is a folk charm for a bountiful harvest," says Madeleine Pelner Cosman in *Medieval Holidays and Festivals* (Charles Scribner's Sons, 1981). Wassailers who drank wassail while wassailing might also toast each other with a joyous "Wassail!"

B Emily Dickinson.

C Mother Goose. Readers may be amused to know that the early nursery chapbook *Mother Goose Melody or Sonnets for the Cradle* put little morals or maxims at the end of each verse. Rather sternly, "High diddle, diddle" concludes with: "It must be a little dog that laughed, for a great dog would be ashamed to laugh at such nonsense."

D Thomas Lovell Beddoes. The answer came easily to the nineteenth-century poet who declares in "Dream Pedlary," "A cottage lone and still/.../ Were dreams to have at will/.../This would I buy."

E Alexander Pope. From "The Rape of the Lock."

F Samuel Taylor Coleridge. From "Frost at Midnight."

G The modern spelling of *ghost* was being used by the end of the sixteenth century. *Goblin* comes from the name of the spirit Gobelinus, who haunted the neighborhood of Evreux in the twelfth century. But *gremlin* must be a modern word. Not found in the *Oxford English Dictionary*, it is defined by *Webster's New World* as "an imaginary small creature humorously blamed for the faulty operation of airplanes or the disruption of any procedure." It comes from the Danish word *graemling*, for imp, and is related to the Old English word *gremian*, "to enrage."

H Mother Goose. *Halloween* comes from the words *All-hallow even*. The *Oxford English Dictionary* notes, "In the Old Celtic calendar the year began on 1st November, so that the last evening of October was 'old-year's night,' the night of all the witches, which the Church transformed into the Eve of All Saints." *Hallow* meant "saint," and still means "to make holy or sacred."

I Mother Goose.

J William Hazlitt. The essayist liked to walk alone, with no particular destination. In "On Going a Journey" he praises the refreshment of solitary rambles. Samuel Johnson defines *journey* as "the travel of a day."

ZEPHYRS

And on the balmy zephyrs tranquil rest

The silver clouds

Z

Yesternight

Yesternight the sun went hence,
And yet is here today....

Y

X marks the spot.

X

WILD

Ring out, wild bells, to the wild sky.

W

VILLAGE

V